MISSA

A CELEBRATION IN

SOLEMNIS
POETRY FOR THREE VOICES

ROBLEY WHITSON

books
1994

Missa Solemnis
by Robley Whitson

Library of Congress Catalog Card Number

93-087687

International Standard Book Number

1-55605-235-9

QH Books
Cloverdale Corporation
Bristol, IN 46507-9460

Printed in the United States of America

TABLE OF CONTENTS

for
John H. Morgan

FOREWORD

Images sounded through words— the poetry of vision in the ultimate power of words...

Body gesture, space filled with light and color, and especially words and music— all these modes of sense, together with the whole range of consciousness integral to them, are the tangibles of the Solemn Mass, *Missa Solemnis*, of the Roman tradition of liturgy.

They make concrete the paradox of the Mystery the liturgy celebrates: the Union of the Divine with the Human— the Transcendent at-one with the phenomenal, or, in traditional Christian terms, God incarnate in an actual human being, God-in-Christ the God-Man. The human bodily reality of sense-brain-mind is the necessary way of entry. Put boldly, God is present with us in a truly human way, the only way possible if Incarnation is real and actually embraces all of us as we are: alive bodily.

The great musical compositions of the Solemn Mass have been able to create sense symbols that open the consciousness of hearers to listen intensely beyond the confines of the liturgical texts. Poetic composition can move the highly focused expressions of the texts into the dimension of image symbol. This is not a reinterpretation or elaboration of text, but a further sense of vision— a realization of how much more there is that the text initiates but cannot exhaust.

The poetry of words as forms, as sounds, as symbols...

Poetry, like music its twin, invites us to experience a special sense of grandeur, or simplicity, or awe, or love, or indeed of any of the intense personal responses that inevitably arise when we are set free. The poetry of this Missa Solemnis, then, seeks to let loose the ultimate power of words— in the beauty of their sound, of the rhythms of phrases, of their feel for reality through image.

The parts of the Mass usually set to music are here set to poetry: the *Kyrie, Gloria, Credo, Sanctus, Agnus Dei*. (The liturgical text, Latin and English, prefaces each of these sections.) In addition there is poetry for an *Introit* as the verse opening a Mass; an *Evangelium* or Gospel scripture reading and discourse; a *Canon* or great prayer of the Eucharist itself; a *Pater Noster* as the Lord's Prayer preparing the community for Communion; and a concluding *Ite Missa Est* whereby the blessing of the celebrated Eucharist is sent out into the world through the community gathered and now dispersing.

As no phenomenal expression can actually represent the Absolute Other of the Transcendent, the poetry constantly plays upon images as seemingly contradictory— as paradoxes proclaiming the Mystery. Some images recur in several sections, often in ways contrary to a previous appearance. In other instances images/words are taken back to their original ancient meanings to restore their experiential impact.

The poetry is designed for choral recitation in three voices (as indicated by the three columns— with the center column as the leading or dominant voice). This three-fold consciousness at times is contrapunctal expressing opposing tensions. At times it is complementary or expansive. At times it moves from the human phenomenal toward the Divine Transcendental. All of these, however, are always intended to free consciousness through the ever more complex and subtle dynamic of symbols, so that what the innermost Reality of the Mass seeks to manifest might be felt, experienced.

> *...Be filled with the Spirit*
> *speaking within yourselves*
> *in psalms and hymns and spiritual songs,*
> *singing and chanting in your heart...*
> (Ephesians 5:18-19)
> *God is Spirit,*
> *and those who worship*
> *must worship in Spirit and Truth.*
> (John 4:24)

INTROIT

Lux hodie:

Light

Today.

The night is over

the True Light already shines.

God is Light,
there is no darkness in God.

As we walk in that Light

we are at one together.

Natus Dominus:

the Lord

born.

Whoever believes
has been begotten by God.

Whoever loves
loves the child begotten.

We know the Son of God has come,

has given us Power
to know the True One.

We are in the True One
as we are in the Anointed Son.

This is the True God,
the Eternal Life.

KYRIE

Kyrie eleison.

Lord have mercy.

Christe eleison.

Christ have mercy.

Kyrie eleison.

Lord have mercy.

Kyrie

eleison

Lord

mercy.

Lord—

the one who owns,
in his hands everything,
the Lord who can provide

Father—

the one who has himself,
himself in another,
the Father who can share.

Gift,
who keeps nothing back
needs nothing
who gives himself away—

Free Gift

Truly Given

Begetting

One

Only

Gift always Given.

Christe

eleison

Christ

mercy.

The Anointed

yesterday

today

beginning

end

all time

all ages

Alpha, Omega.

the Image
of the Unseen

First-born before all
the Gift Given for all

only through him
have all come.

The beginning,

the First-born

from the dead.

All the Fullness
alive in him

raising him high

        drawing all to him

who is the All

        and in all—

    now with that Name,
    the Name beyond all names.

————

    Kyrie

eleison

    Lord

        mercy.

    Spirit
    Breath
    Mother of the living.

The Wisdom of God.

        The Breathed Mystery.

Receive the Breath—
She reaches into everything,

into all the Depths
the very Depths of God,

to know God
from within God.

We have an Anointing
from the Holy One,
the Anointing teaching us
all there is.

Taught in the Spirit

Loving Mother

by Words of Spirit

our own Breath

to recognize God
as God really is:
Giving

in us

always Giving

through us.

Given Once

the Anointed Son.

Ever Giving

the Anointing Spirit.

———————

Kyrie

the Lord is Spirit,
where that Life-Breath is

Christe

all becoming
the Image we see.

Kyrie.

GLORIA

Gloria in excelsis Deo
et in terra pax hominibus bonæ voluntatis.

Glory to God in the utmost heights
and on earth peace to people of good will.

Laudamus te. Benedicimus te.
Adoramus te. Glorificamus te.

We praise you. We bless you.
We adore you. We glorify you.

Gratias agimus tibi propter magnam gloriam tuam.

We give you thanks for your great glory.

Domine Deus, Rex cælestis, Deus Pater omnipotens.

Lord God, heavenly King, God almighty Father.

Domine Fili Unigenite, Jesu Christe.

Lord Only-begotten Son, Jesus Christ.

Domine Deus, Agnus Dei, Filius Patris.

Lord God, Lamb of God, Son of the Father.

Qui tollis peccata mundi,
miserere nobis.
Qui tollis peccata mundi,
suscipe deprecationem nostram.
Qui sedes ad dexteram Patris,
miserere nobis.

You who take away the sins of the world,
have mercy on us.
You who take away the sins of the world,

receive our prayer.
You who sit to the right of the Father,
have mercy on us.

Quoniam tu solus Sanctus. Tu solus Dominus.
Tu solus Altissimus, Jesu Christe.

For you alone are the Holy One. You alone are Lord.
You alone are the Most High, Jesus Christ.

Cum Sancto Spiritu,
in gloria Dei Patris. Amen!

With the Holy Spirit,
in the glory of God the Father. Amen!

Gloria in excelsis
et in terra Pax

Glory in the highest

on earth Peace.

All once far away
are now brought near.

He is our Peace
making two into one
in his own flesh.

And he came proclaiming
Peace to those far off,
Peace to those near at hand.

We bless:

Blest be the God and Father
of our Lord the Anointed
who has blessed us
with every spiritual blessing!

We adore:

In him we were chosen
before the world even began
as his own offspring
to praise the Glory of his Gift
in the One he loves.

We glorify:
God who at the beginning said:

Let light shine out of darkness—
who now shines within our hearts
to be our own radiance
of the Glory ablaze
on the face of the Anointed.

We give you thanks

for your great Glory!

We have been given
the living Glory
that we may be One

so completely One
that our world will realize
God has come in the flesh:

God in One in all

for in him lives bodily

all the Fullness of the Godhead

and we have been completely filled.

Lord God

Celestial King

God Omnipotent Father
Anointed Lord
Only-begotten Son

Lord God

Lamb of God

Son of the Father

You take away
the sins of the world.

You take up
the sins of the world.

You take upon yourself
all the wrongs
our rejections
our unloving

mean and jealous

boastful, conceited

rude and selfish

resentful

all taken by One
always patient and kind
ever rejoicing in the Truth.

And this is the Truth:

Love one another!

Because Love is of God
and everyone who loves
has been begotten by God
and knows God.

Anyone who does not love

        does not know God

    for God is Love.

You take away
the sins of the world.

        You raise up
        all that we seek

    as you are fully able to save
    those who come to God through you,
    for you ever live
    to intercede for all.

    Enthroned

at the right

        of the Father.

    Exalted

come forth from God
into our human life,

    become One with us,

        returning into God
        bringing us with you.

    All of us given in you,
    with you where you are,
    seeing your Glory
    receiving that Glory
    as our own.

Father, glorify your Son

        that your Son may glorify you.

    Only you are Holy

Holy   Holy

    Holy in the Truth.

Proclaim Holy the Name:

        the Only True One

    the Name beyond names.

    Only you are Lord

Lord
beyond all rule and authority

        Lord
        beyond all power and domination.

    Only you are All Highest

Highest   Highest

    Cross, lifted up
    drawing all together—

buried together

        raised together.

You emptied yourself

        but God raises you high

    Savior
    the Anointed

with the Holy Spirit in Glory

        in the Glory of God the Father.

Amen!   Amen!   Amen!

EVANGELIUM

Evangelium
Gospel
Good News

Glad Tidings

        of Great Joy

———————

Search among all the dreamers
for one who looks away from earth
into the glowing hole of the sky,

for one who already knows
there are no visions
in a daylight world
where there is too much to see,

        but only in the night
        stretched out
        scrawled all over
        with starpoint letter words.

Send a messenger into his eyes
one evening as the last of the sun
fades through all its glowing shades
and the first few bright lights
shine faintly in the not yet night.
Tell the messenger to see:
Birth-star.

An alien prophet
to an alien king:
The oracle of the one
with far-seeing eyes,
who hears the Message,
who knows the Knowledge,
who sees all Shaddai makes him see.
I see him, but not now,
I see him, but not near:
A star rises,
a sceptered Ruler.

New prophets
must tell new kings:
We saw his star
rising in the East,
and we have come
to adore the newborn.
We bear King-God treasures
to lay before him
when we find him
in the splendor
of his star-lit house.

The messenger in the dreamer's eyes
must look again and realize
there is nothing of treasure or splendor
written for this new child—
kings and kingdoms,
thrones and crowns,
world wealth and its world of power
are but milky blur visions
of the near blind.

The endless lines of stars are worlds,

countless worlds
open for all to see,

worlds like this one,
homes to peoples.

This is the secret
of those glowing words:

People everywhere,
streaming throughout universes,

looking, seeing worlds
which cannot see—

So knowing,
naked within themselves,
that all worlds
and all things of worlds
are fire and dust,
not treasure and splendor.
Only those with power to see
can come to recognize the wonder
they alone ever are.

Glory!
The skies proclaim it—
each day, each night
heralds it to the next.
Yet there is no
speech or word or sound.
Glory! The star arcs declare it,
reaching through all worlds,
over all the earth.
Glory!

Shepherds in the fields at watch—
outcast from village or house,
animal families
in sheep-pen hovel homes.
Shepherds unlettered in
the stately Way of the Law—
unhallowed by fasts and feasts,
ignorant of the precepts of life,
impure, unclean, despised.
These are the ones
who look up to Glory,
the only ones to hear
the News of Great Joy,
Joy to be shared
with all the worthless:

A child is born,
the one who sets free,
the Anointed—
a swaddled baby in a manger,
the Glory of the All-Highest!

They know they have the power
to see a newborn laid in straw,
dropped into life
as they had been.

They can recognize this marvel:
Now, one of themselves,
the All in all of them.

———

Listen—
hear their tears.
Every day and night
for a thousand thousand years
helpless women have watched
their children wrenched away
out of life barely begun—

Some silently breathless
some choking on their cries

                    some asleep caught unknowing
                    some with fright-widened eyes—

and how many see someone,
not a something,
killing, uncaring!

Send a messenger
into those mothers' tears
not to dry them
nor turn them into laughter,
but to gather them together into oceans,
a Deep over the earth
where no Spirit hovers
breathing their grief.
Tell the messenger to reveal:

Darkness,

            hands closed around something,
            holding tight.
            And in all those tears of Darkness
            have the messenger reveal:

                    Light,

gripping hands able to open,
giving.

The man took the woman for himself.
She bore a son and laughed:
Now I possess my own man!
So she named him Cain, possessed.
But in him murder began,
the rage to seize,
to beat out of life
any other with hands
reaching, taking, keeping.

> All these brothers and sisters
> were fathers and mothers
> generation upon generation.
> People in all their kinds
> wandered out over the earth
> in thousands and millions,
> everywhere grasping everything,
> driving each other away
> with the rage of death.

But from the very first
one message has been
in everyone's heart:
Love one another!
Even the throat-slitters know it.
They say they love some,
then they know how to love any.

> They say they love their own
> but next moment they are liars—
> let even their own reach out
> to take something they want
> and the murdering begins again.
> Someone killed for something.

But there is someone
who is himself the Message,
whose hands never close,
who freely gives himself alive
to all those fearfully clutching
in the darkness of killing.
To all those who grab hold
he gives Eternal Power
to open their hands—

to let go,

to be free!

———————

Out there on the desert edge
where the salt sea shimmers,
a wild prophet messenger
roams and roars in the oven heat
maddened with the vision:
Now he comes!

How many generations
will stumble out their lives
searching face after face
for some inner sign
at last betraying someone
as This One!

Why can they not learn?
No one is coming—
no one will save them
from themselves, from each other.

> No one will free them
> from their waking-dream terror:
> Divine wrath fulloverflowing
> their clay pot lives!

No one is coming.
No one can ever come—
He is already here.
He is always here.

> From the fire and dust
> of a great burst star
> a sun and planets
> swirl into their paths
> and another sphere for life
> begets sense, then mind,
> then vision from within.

There are countless such earths,
each centered on a sun,
each alive with people.

> All of them feel,
> some of them know,
> a few see.

> For every world of people
> there must be one among them
> who is the Vision,
> who is the One
> they all really are

when at last
their dust falls away,

> when finally
> their fire is cold.

> The worlds bring to birth
> all the peoples in all their kinds
> but cannot be their life.

They must escape the dead
walls of worlds made of things
or perish with them.

> They must somehow become Other
> to a self of things.

> And in every world
> there is always One Other,
> the Other in their midst,
> the One who strips things away
> unveiling the already who-we-are.

At first but few see.

> There are only some who know.

> Yet all of us feel
> the ache in hands
> more and more tired
> holding on to everything.
> Grasping hand-fists
> striking out driving others away
> can open—

and fear falls
with all the things
we think we need
to be.

God said the deed:
Let light burst out of dark!
This same God radiates Light,
the Light of Glory,
Glory from within us—
the Face of the Only One.

And those who walk in darkness
in lands of black shadow
see in the Light
the child always born for us:

Wonder
Counsellor
Mighty God
Eternal Father
Prince of Peace—

One
urging
mightily
always
Peace!

One	One	One
urging	urging	urging
mightily	mightily	mightily
always	always	always
Peace!	Peace!	Peace!

CREDO

Credo in unum Deum Patrem omnipotentem

I believe in one God the Almighty Father

Factorem cæli et terræ,
visibilium omnium et invisibilium.

the Maker of heaven and earth,
all that is seen and unseen.

Et in unum Dominum Jesum Christum,
Filium Dei unigenitum.

And in one Lord Jesus Christ,
the only-begotten Son of God.

Et ex Patre natum ante omnia sæcula.

And in him born from the Father before all ages.

Deum de Deo, lumen de lumine,
Deum verum de Deo vero.

God from God, light from light,
true God from true God.

Genitum, non factum,
consubstantialem Patri:
per quem omnia facta sunt.

Begotten, not created,
of the same nature as the Father:
through whom everything was made.

Qui propter nos homines,
et propter nostram salutem
descendit de cælis.

*Who for us and for our salvation
came down from the heavens.*

Et incarnatus est
de Spiritu Sancto ex Maria Virgine:
et homo factus est.

*And was made flesh
by the Holy Spirit from Mary the Virgin:
and became man.*

Crucifixus etiam pro nobis:
sub Pontio Pilato passus,
et sepultus est.

*He was crucified for us:
under Pontius Pilate he suffered
and was buried.*

Et resurrexit tertia die,
secundum Scripturas.

*And he arose on the third day,
fulfilling the Scriptures.*

Et ascendit in cælum:
sedet ad dexteram Patris.

*And he ascended to heaven:
he sits enthroned at
the right of the Father.*

Et iterum venturus est cum gloria
judicare vivos et mortuos:
cujus regni non erit finis.

*And he will come again with Glory
to judge the living and the dead:
and of his reign there will be no end.*

Et in Spiritum Sanctum,
Dominum, et vivificantem:
qui ex Patre, Filioque procedit.

*And in the Holy Spirit,
Lord and Life-Giver,
who proceeds from the Father and Son.*

Qui cum Patre, et Filio
simul adoratur, et conglorificatur:
qui locutus est per Prophetas.

*Who together with the Father and Son
is adored and glorified:
who has spoken by Prophets.*

Et unam sanctam catholicam et apostolicam ecclesiam.

And one, holy, catholic and apostolic church.

Confiteor unum baptisma in remissionem peccatorum.

I profess one baptism for the forgiveness of sins.

Et expecto resurrectionem mortuorum.
Et vitam venturi sæculi.   Amen!

*And I look toward the resurrection of the dead
and the life of the coming Age.   Amen!*

Credo
in Unum
Deum Patrem
Omnipotentem

Blest,

      I believe

            by Gift.

      Believe in One:

in One God

            in God who is One

whole, indivisible,

            the only Fullness

      the Fullness of Father
      begetting from within.

One God who is Father

            Father of all Power

      One God and Father

of all, over all

            through all, in all

      the only Power
      from whom come

the deep of the heavens,
all wandering within it,

                the round of the earth,
                everything and everyone,

all we can see

                all we cannot see.

          I believe
          in One
          God Self-Given
          once for all

Having seen
I believe

                I believe
                without seeing.

          The only Power giving
          All the Father is
          in One Lord
          the Anointed

only-begotten

          from the Father

                born before all time.

God from God

        Light from Light

     True God from True God

begotten from the Father
uncreated

          same as the Father
          in Mystery

      the only Power
      through whom were made
      all, everything, everyone.

God so loves our world

      God gives

         that we might live.

Descending from heaven
coming down from exaltation—

          Coming forth from within Mystery
          emptying himself of Glory—

      Incarnate
      through the Spirit

begotten through the Breath of God
the Living Spirit—

      Incarnate
      through a woman

born from her body
the Mother Virgin—

Incarnate
a man

flesh and blood
alive

in everything like us
alive.

And this is Eternal Life:

that we know
the only True God

and the Anointed
the One sent.

In him is Life,
this Life, our Light,
Light shining in the dark—
that dark
unable to overcome
this Light.

Crucified, suffered

died, buried.

He is in his own world

our world did not know him.

He comes to his own home

we did not receive him.

Rejected, but
he accepts,
gives us Power
to become Offspring of God

not born of blood descent

nor of flesh urge

nor of human will—

Born of God!

In the Breath of Wisdom
enlightening our hearts
we can see the Power—

overwhelming greatness

the strength of true might

raising from the dead

enthroning in Glory—

Power that gives
to us
to our Gathering
to this Body:

the fullness of him

who fills all with the All.

If once we knew
him in the flesh—
no longer!

Anyone in the Anointed
is a new creation.

Old things are no more—

See! they have become new!

He comes now
to the living and the dead.

Live in him!
So as he is revealed
we may have confidence
and not be ashamed
at his appearing.

In this is Love perfected
that we may have confidence
in the day of judgment—
because as he is
so also are we in this world.

There is no fear in Love.
Perfect Love,
the Love God is for us,
casts out all fear.
We love because
God first loves us,

has delivered us
from the dominion of darkness

and brought us into the kingdom
of the Son of his Love—

the joyous and only Ruler,
King of Kings
Lord of Lords,
who alone is immortal
dwelling in inaccessible Light.

———

I believe
in One,
God Self-Giving
always, through all:
the Spirit,
the Living Breath,
Mother

Lord

        Life-Giver

Helper

        Breathing Truth

coming forth from the Father
sent by the Son.

As she comes,
the Spirit of Truth,

        she guides us into all Truth,

and the Anointing we receive
is alive in us

and teaches from within
all that is true.

For all who are guided
by the Spirit of God
are Sons of God—
this Son of God!

And because we truly are,
God sends the Spirit of his Son
into our own hearts
crying out: Abba!

the Spirit of our adoption
our Breath
by whom we cry out: Abba!

The Spirit herself,

our Life-Breath,

our Mother in God,

bears witness
together with our own spirit:
This Truth—
We are Offspring of God!

The Spirit
who bears witness,

who bears us
into Anointed Life

the Spirit comes with us,
helps in our new-born weakness:
Our Spirit Mother
intercedes for us beyond speech
with birth-groanings.
And the Father knows
the Mind of the Mother Spirit.

Father, Son, Spirit:

Gift, Given, Giving.

One Only
adored, glorified
in One New Human Being
in One Body—

baptized through death into Life
called, made holy, glorified—

the one Sanctuary, living Temple
not built by human hands—

the dwelling place of God
in the Spirit
our deep-most Breath.

We have heard
we have seen

we have beheld
we have touched

the Word of Life!
Who is from the beginning

the Mystery so long hidden

but now laid wide open,

the Mystery proclaimed
in all Wisdom:
The Mystery who is
Christ-in-us.

We know
not death, not life
not angels, not rulers

nothing present or yet to come
no powers
neither height nor depth

no creature at all
can ever separate us
from the Love of God
Incarnate,
the Mystery who is
God-in-Christ-in-us:

Anointed Anointed

Anointing. Anointing.

SANCTUS

Sanctus, Sanctus,
Sanctus Dominus
Deus Sabaoth.

Holy, Holy,
Holy Lord
God Sabaoth.

Pleni sunt cæli et terra Gloria tua.

The heavens and the earth are filled
with your Glory.

Hosanna in excelsis!

Hosanna in the utmost heights!

Benedictus qui venit in Nomine Domini.

Blest is he who comes in the Name of the Lord.

Hosanna in excelsis!

Hosanna in the utmost heights!

Sanctus

Holy   Holy

Sanctus

Holy   Holy

Sanctus Dominus

Holy Lord

Deus Sabaoth

God Sabaoth

Sabaoth
the desert whirlwind

Sabaoth
the sandstorm legions

myriads of dust motes

engulfing

overwhelming

the Power in all the smallest
overcoming even the greatest,
wave upon wave
in the oceans of air,

overcoming the sun
darkened at noon,

overcoming man and beast
bowed down upon the ground.

Heaven and earth
and all that is in between
filled with your Glory!

I saw the Lord God
seated on a high throne
and above him seraphs

winged seraphs flying—
And they called out:
Holy! Holy! Holy!

His Glory fills
all the earth.
Hosanna!

in the highest.   in the highest.

He makes the winds
his messengers
and flames of fire
his servants.

Hosanna! Hosanna! Hosanna!

———

Blest is he who comes
in the Name of the Lord

saying
I will proclaim your Name to them
all truly my own,

saying
see—I and the children
whom God gave to me,

the Only-begotten Son
leading these so many Only-begotten
into his Glory!

For both the One sanctifying

and the ones being sanctified

are all of that
one shared
flesh and blood.

One Father and Mother

begetting and bearing all

now the Only Son,
the radiance of Glory,
the exact Image.

That Image we ourselves see,

that Image we ourselves become

in the All Highest.

Hosanna! Hosanna! Hosanna!

CANON

In the beginning
heavens and earth,
a trackless waste,
a dark covered deep.
And the Breath hovered.

        In the beginning the Word
        Word with God
        God the Word:
        All through Word,
        nothing but through Word.

    Before beginning, beyond beginning—
    No doing, no speaking, no thing.

No then, no now, no when.

        No endless always-present:

    The Eternity of No-time,
    not an ever, not a never.
    Images all impossible—

Breath,

      Word—

    The Alone and no other,
    so none to be image.

One   One

    Only.   Only.

A beginning is our image:

we think
Now
God makes or speaks

        and
        When
        God does

all everything else comes
so the beginning was
Then.

Let light shine!
the deep dark divided,
day and night.

        We imagine two,
        two at odds,
        two warring.
        But at any beginning
        all that could become

radiance sphering out,
black crashing in,
light-torn void

        clouded dust streams,
        star furnaces,
        circle rocks—

Everything was one crush.

All came into life in Word—
life as light in darkness,
light overcoming dark.

It is never war,

light-dark,

bright-dull.

It is a world of worlds
gone out away
from first burst

every one
one at the center,
every one the center
always—

all the others
rushing away,
yet all the others
also that one center—

always thinning out,
out from within,
endlessly,

swirling together
intermingling,

crushing in
endlessly.

Life first pulsed
in echo of light.

Let there be
sky and ocean!
Let there be
sea and land,
seeds and trees!
Let there be
sun and moon,
night and day!

Water and air
fill with creatures!
All the world
fill with beasts of earth,
fill with earth-man, earth-woman!

But this is nothing,
only one more rush
in the tide of things
groping their way
out to nowhere.

Yet some are not the same,
not more mere life,
not bits of all the rest.

Life births
marvellous others
blazing from within

with power—
power not to be part
of endless coming and going.
They contradict:
arisen from everything else

from universe parents

        from crush and burst

    nonetheless

a new self,

       truly a self—

some
one

       not some
       thing.

    None other like this
    One: Only: I—
    all the one-onlys.

———————

       The Word here unknown
       in an unknowing world

belongs with us
the rejectors.

     The countless images,
     old and false selves—

things
as if us,

       fakes
       we make

when we forget
who we really are.
We are other
to this universe
of before-and-after
for we are the one-onlys,
the only ones
fully ourselves—

cannot be else
even when we wish it,

        cannot pretend
        even when we hide.

     This should have been our world
     from the beginning,

our bones and flesh
are formed of it,
but our truth is not.

        There is no self
        in bodies or blood,
        none in light or life.

These are but hints,

        faint signs pointing.

     There is no word for self,
     nothing at all to say
     the mystery
     what-who I am.

———

There in the garden—
do not dare
to take and eat
to try to be Me!
But

> But
> to acceptors
> Power is given—
> to all
> not blood-born,
> not flesh-urged,
> not human-willed—
> the God-begotten!

> And so we dare
> to take and eat!
> Whoever eat
> whoever drink
> live in me

into Eternal Life

> all One with the Other.

> I live in them
> I raise them up

from the last of night

> into this Light at last.

These hinting words
are Spirit
are Breath.

These pointing words
are Life
are Light.

Taking some bread
blessing it
breaking it
giving it—

This is my Body
handed over.

Lifting up the Cup
offering thanks
giving it
all drinking—

This is my Blood
poured out.

Our eyes open,
we recognize,
and vanish from sight.

Our hearts afire,
listening deep within
as we walk the road.

It is true!
We recognize
in the breaking of bread
the Fullness—

Father and Mother

and all the Only-begotten,

Love made visible

        embodied

    the Mystery shared:

the fullness of the

One   One

        filling all with the

   All.   All.

We see Glory,
Only-begotten,
Gift and Truth—
Fullness in us:
Gift upon Gift.

The One-Only God,
the Truth
in our truth—
selves filled to become
all the one-onlys.

    Always unseen
    yet
    made known to all.

Light beyond light—

So not light!

No life, no whatever!

Known, not in mind,
known in the feel
of our own embrace
as we hug to ourselves
all the wonderfilled ones:
I, You— We.

In that feel we see.

And we see

no first-and-last

no one-then-another

no beginning-but-end

no all-thing.

But we can know
at last—

Loved   Loved

Loving.   Loving.

PATER NOSTER

When you pray, say:
Abba!
Kiddush ha-Shem—

Abba:
Our Father

No!
Abba—!

Abba:
Daddy

No hint
of Glory and Majesty,

a child
in loving delight.

Abba—

no awe
of an All-Powerful,

the wonder
of the All-Loving.

Kiddush ha-Shem:
Sanctify the Name

in everything we are
proclaim that Name Holy,

in everything we do
live life in holiness
in that Name of delight.

Then will people see
the Mystery:
Abba in all of us

the way God really is!

The One we can love in delight

in the kingdom

that is a seed
grown to a tree
alive with birds,

in the kingdom

that is a feast,
a wedding of life,
everyone belonging

in the kingdom
that is our Bread
living Bread
life Bread

the kingdom
of forgiveness

the kingdom
of deliverance

the kingdom

of Abba,

of delight.

Amen!

AGNUS DEI

Agnus Dei
qui tollis peccata mundi,
miserere nobis!

Lamb of God
who take away the sins of the world,
have mercy on us!

Agnus Dei
qui tollis peccata mundi,
miserere nobis!

Lamb of God
who take away the sins of the world,
have mercy on us!

Agnus Dei
qui tollis peccata mundi,
dona nobis pacem!

Lamb of God
who take away the sins of the world,
grant us peace!

Agnus Dei

Lamb of God

Lamb who was slain

freeing us all

from every evil.

The Lamb who was slain
is worthy to receive

power and treasure

wisdom and strength

honor and glory and blessing.
Every living creature

in heaven, on earth

within the earth, upon the sea

everything—crying out:

To the One seated upon the Throne

and to the Lamb before the Throne

blessing	blessing	blessing
and	and	and
honor,	honor,	honor,
glory	glory	glory
and	and	and
might,	might,	might,

age

        upon

             age.

Agnus Dei

             Lamb of God

        A crowd vast beyond all counting

every nation and tribe

           every people and tongue

before the Throne and Lamb

           serving day and night.

        And the One enthroned
        will raise the Tabernacle
        his tent over them.

And the Lamb at the Throne
will shepherd them,

           lead them to the fountains
           of the waters of Life,

        the river of Life
        bright as crystal
        rising from the Throne of God
        flowing from the font of the Lamb.

Agnus Dei

Lamb of God

Happy those called to
the wedding feast of the Lamb!

Rejoice and exult,

give glory to him:

The marriage of the Lamb has come!

His Bride has prepared herself

clothed in linen garments
all dazzling bright:

the deeds of the holy ones.

The Spirit and the Bride
say: Come!

Let everyone who hears
say: Come!

Let all the thirsty come.
Let all who wish it
take of the water of Life freely.

And now
a new heaven,
a new earth!

The first heaven and earth—
Gone!

And the sea—
No more!

The Tabernacle of God with us—
God lives with us!

We shall be his people.

He will be our God.

The Lamb: His Peace.

Our Peace.   Our Peace.

ITE MISSA EST

Ite, missa est!
Go! — Sent!

Go forth into all the world
with the blessing of gift.

        Sent to everyone, anyone
        with the gift of blessing.

Today

        Tonight

    Light—
    one ray,

        only one,
        all we need
        to see our way,

a single pace lit
ahead of each footstep.

        Walk or run—
        no difference.

There is always
that much light—

        enough, not more.

    It is dark still
    but the night is over.

There was day once,
sun and warmth—

        Remember, seeing everything,
        all the earth, in a circle.

Before it all faded

        faded off into night.

     And illusions:
     Stars—

stars everywhere

    delusions

        lights that lit nothing

walking blind
stumbling and falling

        hearing yells of pain
        curses, crying, fear.

Looking up through the dark
at all those useless stars

        trying to see everything
        we used to see
        when it was day—

a hunter with a bow
a virgin

                bears and lions

scorpions, serpents

                a gush of milk

       illusions:
       lines of white dots,
       pictures on
       black scrolls of sky.

The lost day,
remembered only.

                The dark night,
                wandered whereless.

       Light—
       one ray.

Night ended, but

                but not day again.

Some other light.

                Light, some other.

       Light not-light
       Light—
       the Other.

Light in the dark

                ahead of each footfall

        Light that says

Come!
Come into Me!

                Come!
                Come all of you!

        Come
        into this

Light!   Light!   Light!

SCRIPTURE SOURCES
Initial Occurence, First Verse

INTROIT	1Jn 2:8	(CREDO)	Jn 17:3
	1Jn 1:5		Jn 1:4
	1Jn 5:20		Eph 1:17
			2Cr 5:16
KYRIE	Rev 1:7		1Jn 2:28
	Col 1:15		1Jn 4:17
	Phl 2:6		Col 1:13
	Col 3:11		1Tm 6:15
	1Cr 2:6		Jn 15:26
	1Jn 2:20		1Jn 2:20
			Rm 8:14
GLORIA	Eph 2:13		Gal 4:6
	Eph 1:3		Rm 8:15
	2Cr 4:6		1Jn 1:1
	Jn 17:22		Rm 8:38
	Col 2:9		
	1Cr 13:4	SANCTUS	Is 6:1
	1Jn 4:7		Ps 104:4
	Heb 7:25		Heb 2:12
	Jn 16:28		Heb 1:3
	Jn 17:24		
	Jn 17:1	CANON	Gen 1:2
	Jn 17:177		Jn 1:1
	Eph 1:21		Gen 2:17
			Mk 14:22
EVANGEL.	Num 24:15		Lk 24:31
	Mtt 2:2		
	Ps 19:1	PATER NR.	Lk 11:2
	Lk 2:8		
	Gen 4:1	AGNUS DEI	Rev 5:6
	1Jn 3:11		Rev 7:9
	2Cr 4:6		Rev 22:1
	Is 9:6		Rev 19:7
			Rev 22:17
CREDO	Eph 4:6		Rev 21:1
	Phl 2:6		